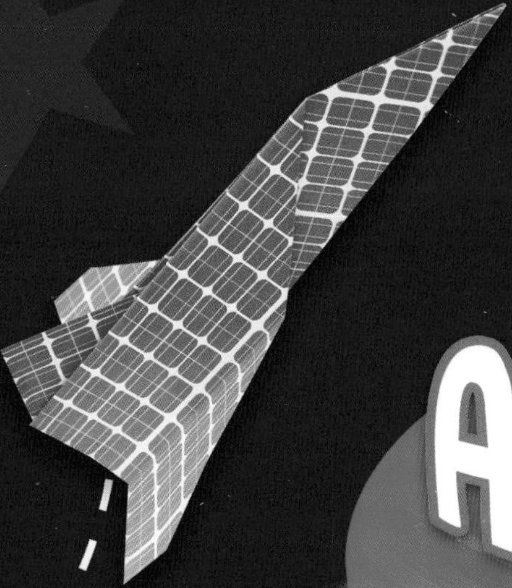

Air-igami

ORIGAMI SPACESHIPS

CATHERINE ARD

PowerKiDS
press

Published in 2019 by
The Rosen Publishing Group, Inc.
29 East 21st Street, New York, NY 10010

Cataloging-in-Publication Data

Names: Ard, Catherine.
Title: Origami spaceships / Catherine Ard.
Description: New York : PowerKids Press, 2019. | Series: Air-ogami | Includes glossary and index.
Identifiers: ISBN 9781538347164 (pbk.) | ISBN 9781538347188 (library bound) | ISBN 9781538347171 (6pack)
Subjects: LCSH: Origami–Juvenile literature. | Space ships in art–Juvenile literature.
Classification: LCC TT872.5 A733 2019 | DDC 736'.982–dc23
Copyright © Arcturus Holdings Ltd, 2019

Models and photography: Michael Wiles
Text: Catherine Ard
Design: Picnic, with Emma Randall
Edited: Kate Overy, with Julia Adams

Manufactured in the United States of America

CPSIA Compliance Information: Batch #CWPK19:
For Further Information contact
Rosen Publishing, New York, New York
at 1-800-237-9932.

Contents

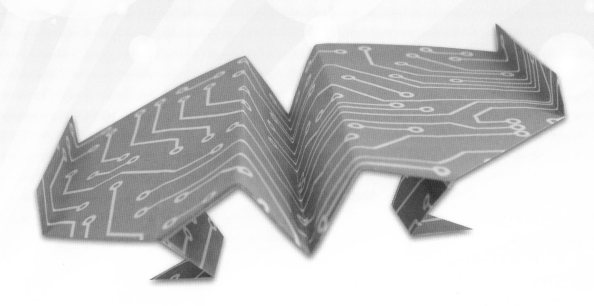

Basic folds

This book shows you how to make a fantastic fleet of paper spaceships. All you need for each model is a sheet of paper, your fingers, and some clever creasing. So, get folding and get flying!

GETTING STARTED

The paper we've used for these spaceships is thin but strong, so that it can be folded many times. You can use ordinary scrap paper, but make sure it's not too thick.

A lot of the spaceships in this book are made with the same folds. The ones that appear most are explained on these pages. It's a good idea to try out these folds before you start.

KEY

When making the spaceships, follow this key to find out what the lines and symbols mean.

.... mountain fold

--- --- --- --- --- valley fold

➤ direction to move paper

◀ ▶ direction to push or pull paper

MOUNTAIN FOLD

To make a mountain fold, fold the paper so that the crease is pointing up at you, like a mountain.

VALLEY FOLD

To make a valley fold, fold the paper the other way, so that the crease is pointing away from you, like a valley.

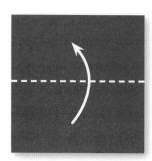

OUTSIDE REVERSE FOLD

An outside reverse fold can be used to create a spaceship's nose.

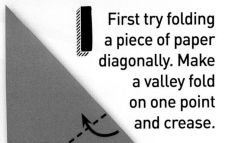

1 First try folding a piece of paper diagonally. Make a valley fold on one point and crease.

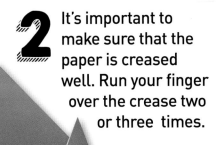

2 It's important to make sure that the paper is creased well. Run your finger over the crease two or three times.

3 Unfold and open up the corner slightly. Refold the crease farthest away from you into a valley fold.

4 Open up the paper a little more and start to turn the corner inside out. Then close the paper when the fold begins to turn.

5 OPEN

You now have an outside reverse fold. You can either flatten the paper or leave it rounded out.

FOLDING TIPS

Paper spaceships are easy to make, and fun to fly, but you need to fold with care if your models are going to glide, loop, twirl, and dive the way they are meant to.

1 Before you crease the paper, make sure the edges, or points, meet exactly where they are supposed to. Even small overlaps will make the spaceship hard to fly.

2 Use a ruler to help you line up your creases, especially when you are folding a sharp nose point, or creasing several layers of paper at once.

USE A RULER!

3 The left side of the model is always a mirror image of the right side of the model. Carefully line up the second wing to match the first wing.

4 Before you fly a spaceship, check that the wings and wing tips are sitting at the same angle on each side. Crooked wings won't fly!

Nebula

Get on a roll with this easy-to-fold tube, then test the laws of gravity when you send it spinning through space!

CURL AND WHIRL!

1 Place the paper as shown. Fold it in half from top to bottom and unfold.

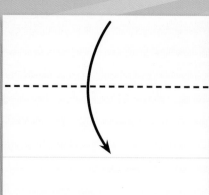

2 Fold the top edge down to meet the center crease.

3 Fold the flap in half from top to bottom.

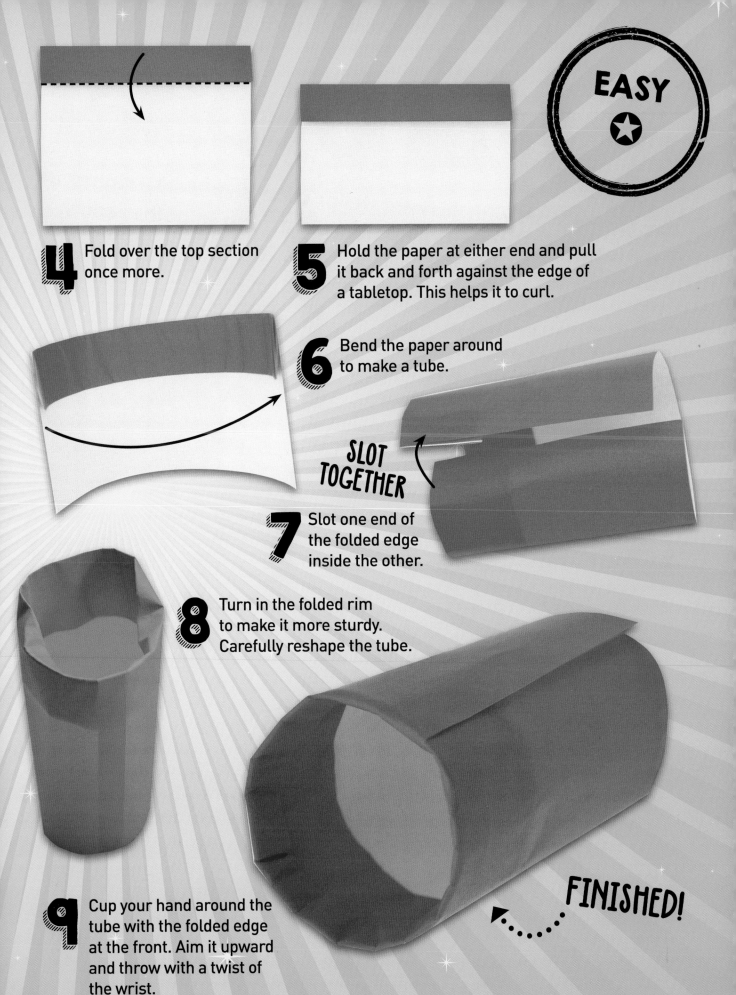

4 Fold over the top section once more.

5 Hold the paper at either end and pull it back and forth against the edge of a tabletop. This helps it to curl.

6 Bend the paper around to make a tube.

SLOT TOGETHER

7 Slot one end of the folded edge inside the other.

8 Turn in the folded rim to make it more sturdy. Carefully reshape the tube.

9 Cup your hand around the tube with the folded edge at the front. Aim it upward and throw with a twist of the wrist.

FINISHED!

Astral Orbiter

Aim for the stars with this interstellar spaceship! Fold it right and it will loop in midair before floating down for a smooth reentry.

LUNAR LOOPS!

1 Place the paper as shown. Valley fold it in half from left to right and unfold.

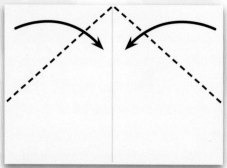

2 Valley fold the top edges to meet on the center crease.

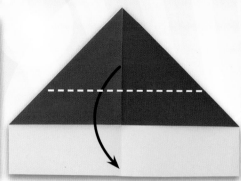

3 Now valley fold the point to meet the bottom edge.

8

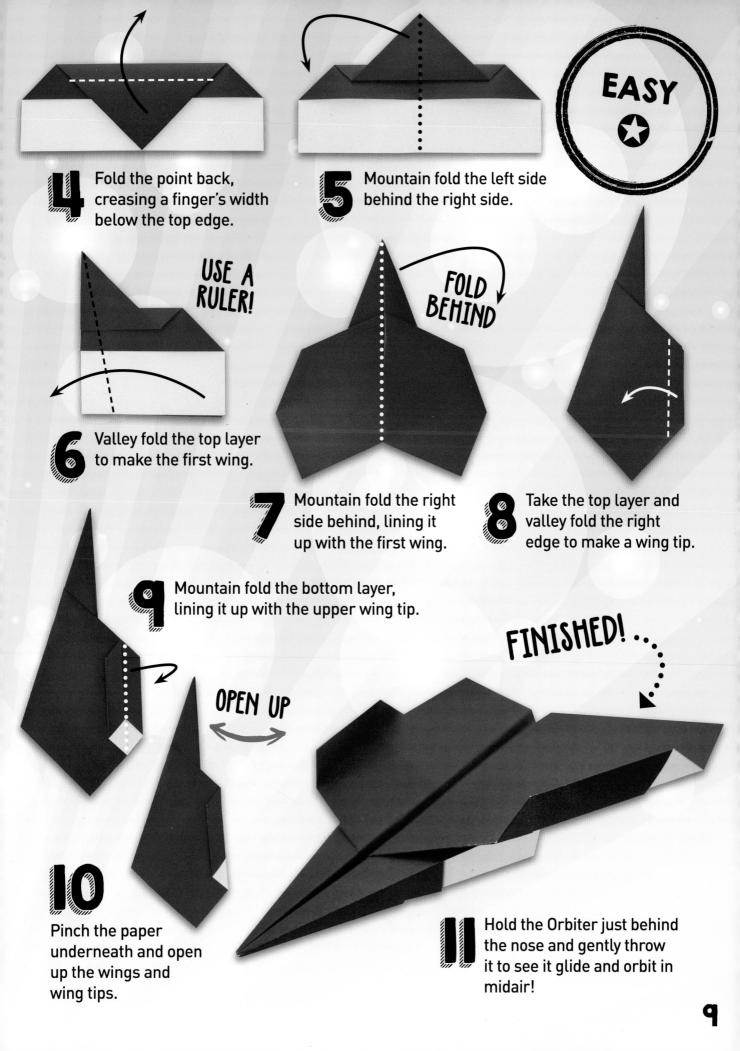

4 Fold the point back, creasing a finger's width below the top edge.

5 Mountain fold the left side behind the right side.

EASY ★

USE A RULER!

FOLD BEHIND

6 Valley fold the top layer to make the first wing.

7 Mountain fold the right side behind, lining it up with the first wing.

8 Take the top layer and valley fold the right edge to make a wing tip.

9 Mountain fold the bottom layer, lining it up with the upper wing tip.

FINISHED!

OPEN UP

10 Pinch the paper underneath and open up the wings and wing tips.

11 Hold the Orbiter just behind the nose and gently throw it to see it glide and orbit in midair!

9

Galactic Rover

Fold this cosmic spacecraft with its futuristic nose, then send it soaring into hyperspace with a rocket-powered throw!

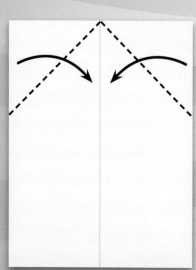 GLIDE AND RIDE!

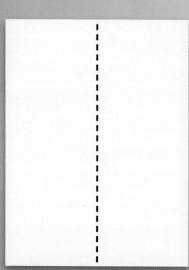

1 Place the paper as shown. Fold it in half from left to right and unfold.

2 Valley fold the top edges to meet on the center crease.

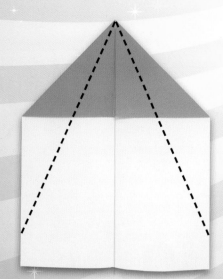

3 Valley fold the sides so that the patterned edges meet on the center crease.

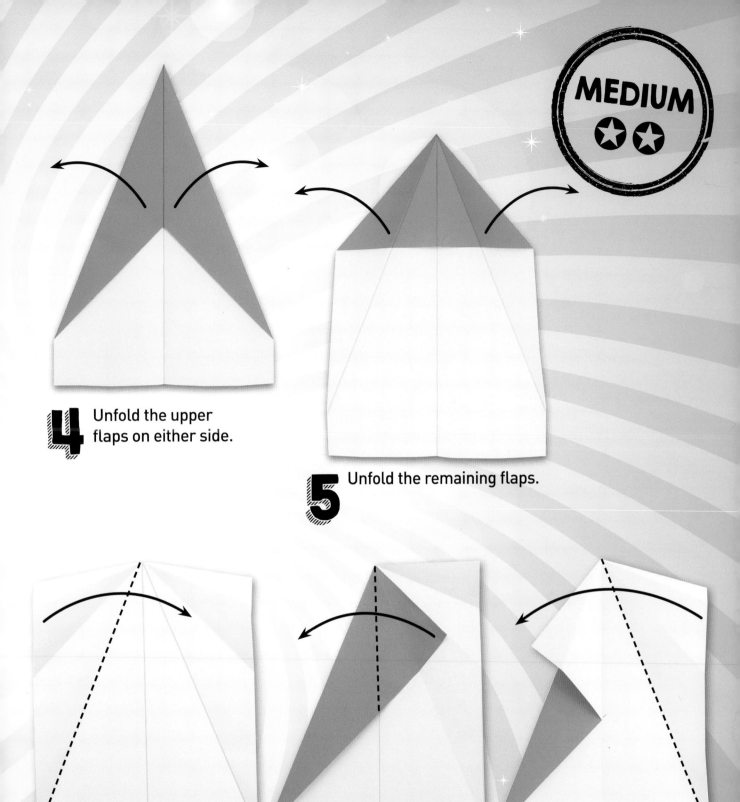

4 Unfold the upper flaps on either side.

5 Unfold the remaining flaps.

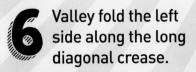 **6** Valley fold the left side along the long diagonal crease.

 7 Fold the left corner back along the middle crease.

 8 Now valley fold the right side along the long diagonal crease.

MEDIUM
⭐⭐

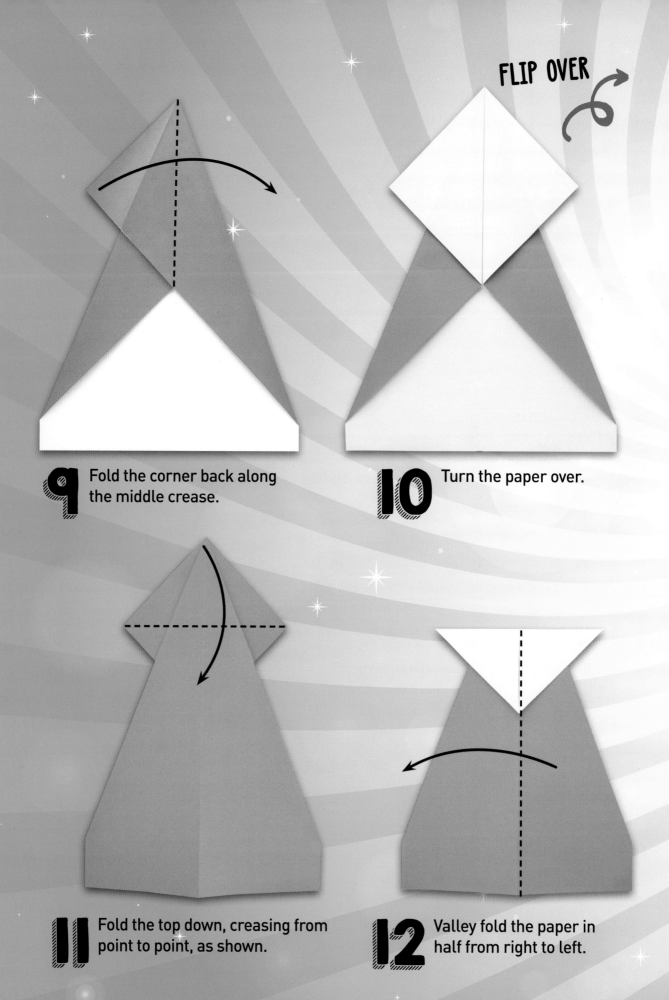

FLIP OVER

9 Fold the corner back along the middle crease.

10 Turn the paper over.

11 Fold the top down, creasing from point to point, as shown.

12 Valley fold the paper in half from right to left.

13

Take the top layer and valley fold it to make the first wing.

FOLD BEHIND

14

Mountain fold the left side behind, lining it up with the first wing.

15

Pinch the paper underneath and pull up the wings.

OPEN UP

NOSE FLAPS

16

Open up the nose flaps to make them rounded.

17

Make sure that the wings are smooth and level, then launch your Galactic Rover with a good, straight throw.

FINISHED!

Lunar Explorer

This neat flyer is perfect for space exploration. Fold out its feet for tricky moon landings, or tuck them in to glide through the galaxy!

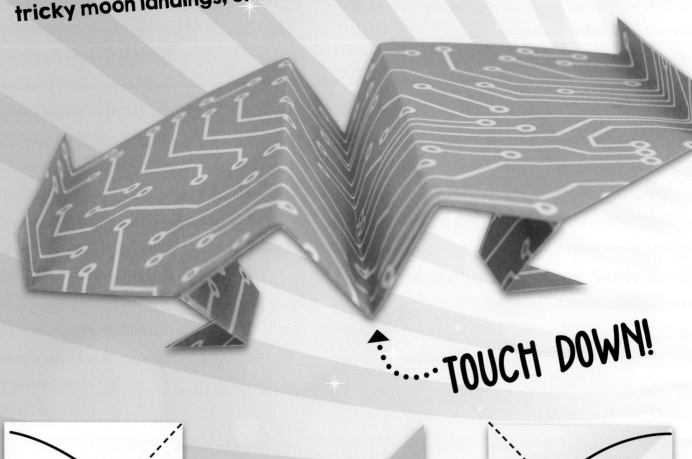

....TOUCH DOWN!

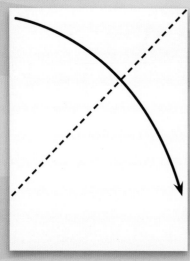

1 Place the paper as shown. Valley fold the top edge to meet the right-hand edge.

2 Open up the paper.

OPEN UP

3 Now valley fold the top edge to meet the left-hand edge.

 OPEN UP

FLIP OVER

4 Open up the paper.

5 You should now have a creased cross. Turn the paper over.

 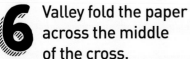 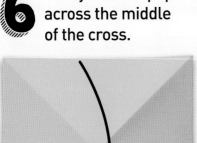

6 Valley fold the paper across the middle of the cross.

7 Open up the paper again.

8 Turn the paper over.

FLIP OVER

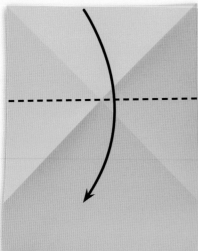

PUSH IN HERE ▼

9 Push in on the central point to make the sides pop up.

10

Push in the sides on the center crease until they collapse.

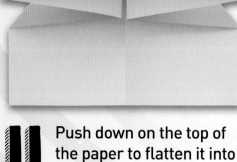

PUSH DOWN HERE

11

Push down on the top of the paper to flatten it into a triangle shape.

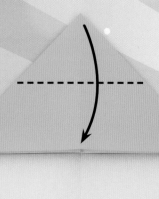

12

Fold down the top point to meet the bottom edge of the triangle. Crease firmly.

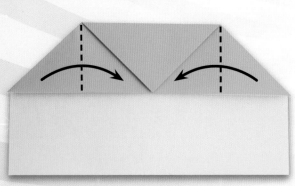

13

Take the top layer and fold in the flaps on either side to make an envelope shape.

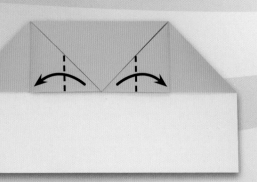

14

Fold back the flap points to meet the edges of the envelope.

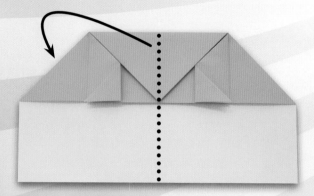

15

Mountain fold the left side behind the right side.

16

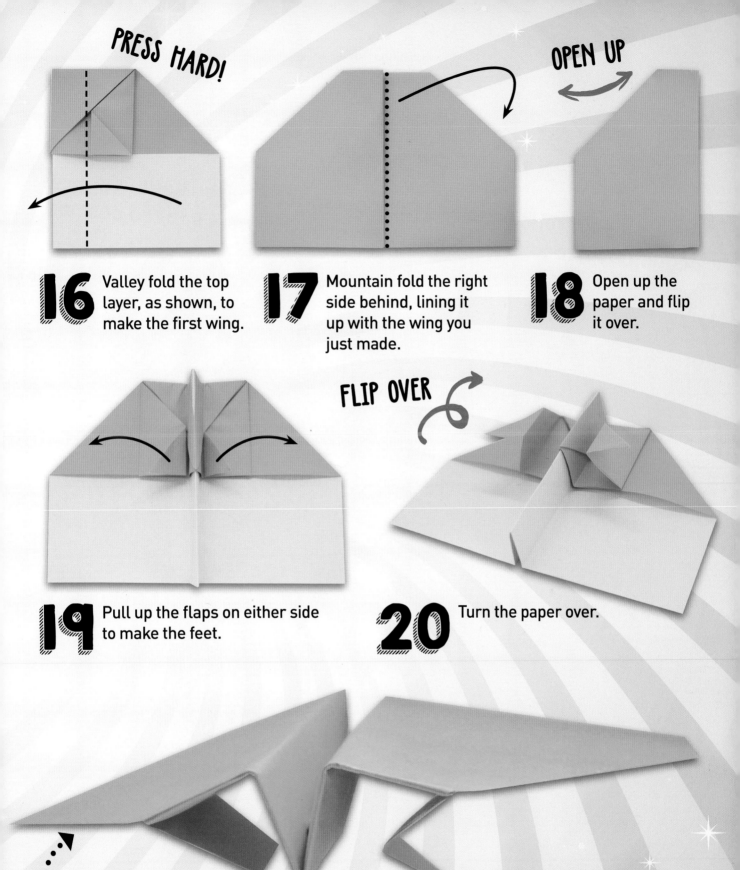

PRESS HARD!

OPEN UP

16 Valley fold the top layer, as shown, to make the first wing.

17 Mountain fold the right side behind, lining it up with the wing you just made.

18 Open up the paper and flip it over.

FLIP OVER

19 Pull up the flaps on either side to make the feet.

20 Turn the paper over.

FINISHED!

21 Pinch the Lunar Explorer underneath and throw it gently forward. It will swoop and then come in to land on its feet!

Space Shuttle

Make it your mission to fold this cool space cruiser. Begin the countdown to takeoff, then send it corkscrewing into the cosmos!

BLAST OFF!

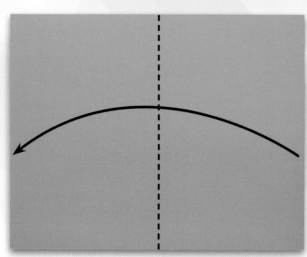

1 Place the paper with the white side down. Fold it in half from right to left.

2 Make an angled valley fold across the bottom right-hand corner.

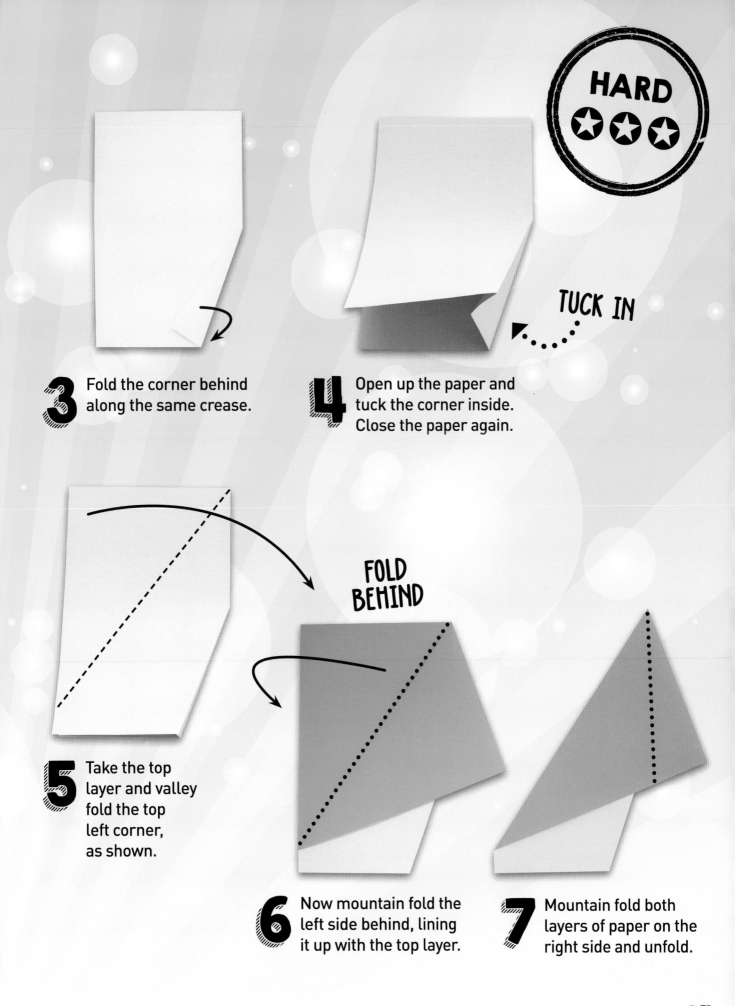

3 Fold the corner behind along the same crease.

4 Open up the paper and tuck the corner inside. Close the paper again.

TUCK IN

5 Take the top layer and valley fold the top left corner, as shown.

FOLD BEHIND

6 Now mountain fold the left side behind, lining it up with the top layer.

7 Mountain fold both layers of paper on the right side and unfold.

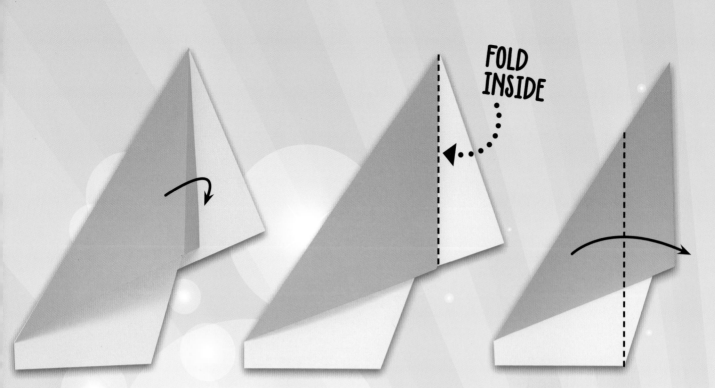

FOLD INSIDE

8 Fold the top layer inside along the crease you just made.

9 Fold the bottom layer inside along the crease.

10 Fold back the top layer, as shown.

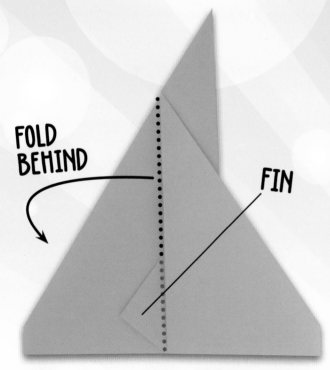

FOLD BEHIND

FIN

11 Mountain fold the left side behind, leaving the fin sticking out. Line up the top and bottom layers exactly.

NOSE

12 Valley fold the top layer in line with the nose section. This makes the first wing.

TURN 90°

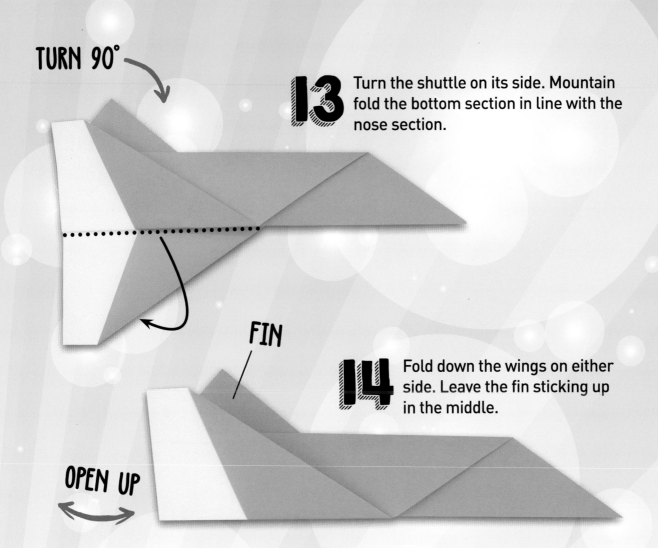

13 Turn the shuttle on its side. Mountain fold the bottom section in line with the nose section.

FIN

14 Fold down the wings on either side. Leave the fin sticking up in the middle.

OPEN UP

15

Hold the shuttle just in front of the wings and send it spinning into space with a strong, upward throw.

FINISHED!

Alien Invader

Look out, the Martians are coming! This stealthy UFO swoops silently overhead before diving down for a close encounter!

DRIFT AND DIVE!

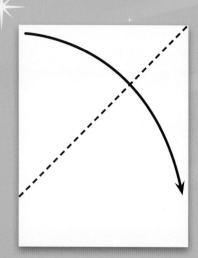

OPEN UP

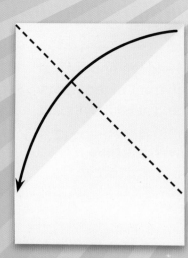

1 Place the paper as shown. Valley fold the top edge to meet the right-hand edge.

2 Open up the paper.

3 Now valley fold the top edge to meet the left-hand edge.

OPEN UP

FLIP OVER

4 Open up the paper.

5 You should now have a creased cross. Turn the paper over.

6 Valley fold the paper across the middle of the cross.

7 Open up the paper once more.

8 Turn the paper over.

FLIP OVER

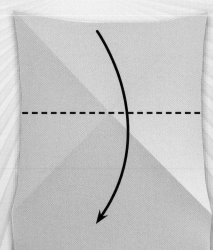

PUSH IN HERE ▼

9 Push in on the central point to make the sides pop up.

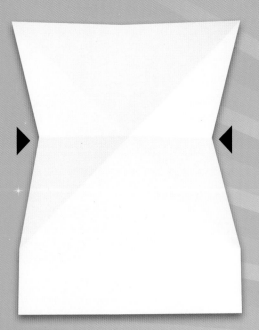

10 Push in the sides on the center crease until they collapse.

11 Push down on the top of the paper to flatten it into a triangle shape.

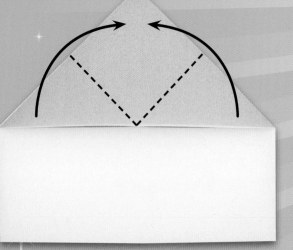

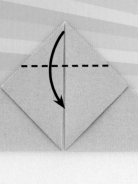

12 Taking the top layer, bring up the bottom points of the triangle to meet the top point.

13 Fold down the top point, as shown.

14 Lift up the flap that you just made.

LIFT
UP

TUCK IN

15 Lift up the bottom left-hand flap.

16 Tuck the folded part of the bottom flap between the layers of the top flap.

PULL OUT

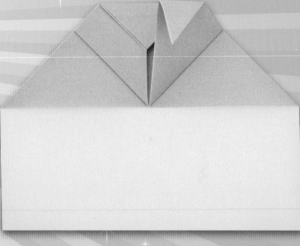

17 Now pull out the bottom right-hand flap.

18 Your paper should look like this.

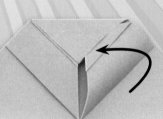
TUCK IN

19 Tuck the folded part of the bottom flap between the layers of the top flap.

25

FLIP OVER

20 Turn the paper over.

21 Valley fold the left side from point to point. Leave the corner sticking out at the top.

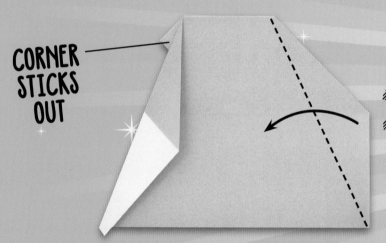

CORNER STICKS OUT

22 Now make a matching valley fold on the other side.

23 Valley fold the left-hand flap, as shown.

24 Make a matching valley fold on the right-hand flap.

POCKET

25 Put your hand inside the pocket underneath. Open up the pocket to give the model a rounded shape.

26 Your spacecraft should look like this. Pull out the wings on either side.

FINISHED!

27 Hold the spacecraft by sliding your hand inside the pocket underneath. Pull back your arm and shoot it forward to send your Alien Invader flying!

The UFO

This Unidentified Flying Object was last seen shooting through the air near you!

1 You need a large circle shape and there are several ways to make one: use a pencil and compass or draw around a circular object, e.g. a lid or roll of tape. Carefully cut out your paper circle.

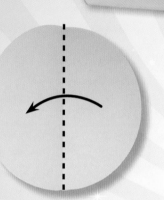

2 Fold the circle in half vertically from right to left. Make sure the edges align so the fold is in the center. Unfold.

3 Fold down the top edge a short way. Make sure the center folds align. Unfold again.

4 Now fold the top left edge, diagonally toward the center. Align the left horizontal fold with the lower vertical fold.

FLIP OVER

5 Repeat step 4 on the top right edge, aligning the right horizontal fold with the lower vertical fold. Unfold to reveal a star shape.

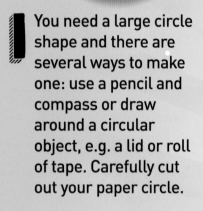

6 Turn the paper over and make the horizontal fold again, using the fold line from step 3. Unfold again.

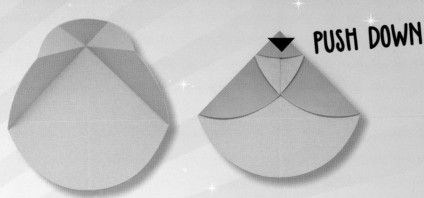

7 Turn the paper back over. The horizontal fold lines will lift up toward you. Pinch each side together, starting on the left side, and press downward so that each horizontal fold line aligns with the lower vertical fold line.

8 When you have pressed the top paper firmly, fold the top left flap in toward the center crease. Unfold. Repeat on the right-hand side. Unfold.

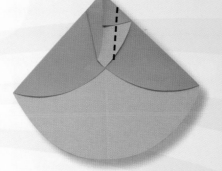

9 Fold the top point downward, using the points of the top folds as a guide for the horizontal crease.

TUCK IN   **FLIP OVER**

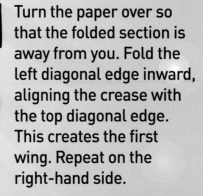

11 Turn the paper over so that the folded section is away from you. Fold the left diagonal edge inward, aligning the crease with the top diagonal edge. This creates the first wing. Repeat on the right-hand side.

10 Carefully tuck the left-hand fold underneath the top flap, which acts as a sort of pocket. Repeat on the right-hand side.

FINISHED!

12 Turn the UFO over so the wing tips face upward. Your strange flying object is ready to take to the alien skies—we come in peace!

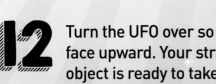

29

Glossary

astral
Relating to the stars.

corkscrew
To twist in a spiral motion.

cosmos
The universe.

fleet
A group of spacecraft that
fly together.

gravity
A force which tries to pull two
objects together. Earth's gravity is
what keeps us on the ground, and
what makes objects fall.

hyperspace
A space with more than three
dimensions. In stories, hyperspace
often allows for time travel.

interstellar
Between stars.

lunar
Relating to a moon.

Martian
Related to Mars; a being that is
supposedly from Mars.

nebula
A cloud of gas and dust in outer
space that is sometimes visible in
the night sky.

reentry
When a spacecraft enters
Earth's atmosphere, returning
from a space mission.

stealthy
To do something in a way that
makes it barely noticeable.

Further Information

Books:

Lee, Kyong Hwa. *Amazing Paper Airplanes: The Craft and Science of Flight*. Albuquerque, NM: University of New Mexico Press, 2016.

Martin, Jerome. *100 Paper Spaceships to Fold and Fly*. London, UK: Usborne, 2015.

Mitchell, David. *Paper Planes: 225 Superdynamic Aeroplanes to Make and Fly*. London, UK: Pavilion Books, 2017.

Robinson, Nick. *The Encyclopedia of Origami Techniques*. Tunbridge Wells, UK: Search Press, 2016.

Szinger, John. *Air and Space Origami: Realistic Paper Rockets, Spaceships and More!* North Clarendon, VT: Tuttle Publishing, 2018.

Websites:

www.scienceforkidsclub.com/paper-airplanes.html
Visit this website to find out all about the science behind paper planes and what makes them fly faster and farther.

https://www.youtube.com/watch?v=7SKkRNwTHXg
A video that shows you how to fold a NASA space shuttle.

Index